Amazon Echo: Dot

The Ultimate User Guide to Amazon Echo Dot 2nd Generation For Newbie (Amazon Echo Dot, user manual, Amazon Echo, tips and tricks, user guide)

ANDREW BUTLER

CONTENTS

Introduction

The Amazon Echo Dot is the smaller version of the Amazon Echo. This second generation release comes in a sleeker design with updated features. One of the updates is a more powerful speech processor. Dot also comes with Echo Spatial Perception (ESP). ESP is used when there are multiple Alexa devices in the same home. However, it ensures that the closest device responds first. The option of placing a Dot in every room is tempting, especially with the bargain that comes with buying 5 and getting 1 free. For the larger home, there is also the option to buy 10 and get 2 free.

In a nutshell, the Amazon Echo Dot is changing the game for smart speakers. This is not your run-of-the-mill Bluetooth device. It does more than just play music. The Amazon Echo Dot is a game changer due to its compact design and small price. This device is able to hold its own against any of its competitors. Playing music isn't the only thing Dot can do—it can call an Uber, order a Domino's pizza, and even control your home. With Alexa being built in the cloud, the device is continuously learning. Updates to Dot are sent automatically. The Echo Dot is smart enough to adapt to speech patterns, personal preferences, and vocabulary.

This device is a powerhouse in a small package. Not only does it fit anywhere, but it comes standard in two colors: black or white. It is also available in various leathers and fabrics to blend in with any environment. The Echo Dot is made for any room. If desired the Dot can be ordered alone or as part of a bundle. These bundle options include being paired with the Bose Soundlink Mini II, the Phillips Hue Starter Kit, the TP-Link Smartplug, or the ecobee3 Smart Thermostat. These add-ons aid in controlling appliances, altering home lighting, and even changing thermostat settings all with the use of your voice.

The device is able to hear you from across any room. It even has the ability to recognize your voice in loud settings or when music is playing. This is all thanks to the seven built-in far-field microphones used for hands-free control. The device awakens simply with the word "Alexa." This is indicated by the lighting of the blue ring on the top of the device as a response to its name.

The Echo Dot has no shortage of capabilities. With Alexa at its core, Dot can be customized with skills that fit your lifestyle. It will aid you in getting things done, checking schedules for the individual who stays on the go, staying informed about current events, and so much more. It is also able to play music through Amazon Music, Spotify, Pandora, iHeartRadio, and TuneIn.

The Amazon Echo Dot is a truly innovative device that gives you all of the pieces of your world in one place. It's simple, intuitive, and sleek. What are you waiting for? Get your Amazon Echo Dot right now!

Chapter 1: Using Your Amazon Echo Dot (Second Generation)

The Amazon Echo Dot is a lot of different things for different users. For some, its intended purpose is to control their home and all of the components in it, whereas for others it is a gadget to make simple mundane tasks more convenient.

The Echo Dot literally looks as if Amazon decided to slice off the top of the Echo and voila! A new and innovative gadget at less than half the price of the original. The second generation Echo Dot is even smaller than its first generation predecessor, yet it still holds true to its puck-like design. This device even allows you to switch effortlessly between wired and Bluetooth speakers by simply disabling Bluetooth connection with the use of your voice.

If you are an avid Amazon Alexa user and have purchased multiple Alexa products, the new Echo Spatial Perception Technology will be just what you need. This technology detects which Echo Dot your voice is interacting with so that all of your devices do not respond at once. This technology will also be rolled out to existing Amazon Echo and Amazon Echo Dot (First Generation) products.

The Echo Dot offers a large variety of options and skills for every user. Below you will find details on some of the functions that the Echo Dot offers and how they can be used.

echo dot

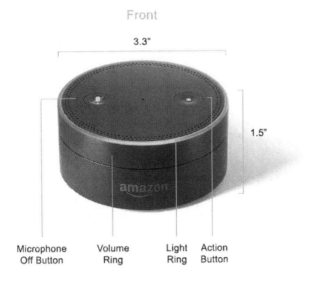

Front

3.3"

1.5"

Microphone   Volume   Light   Action
Off Button   Ring   Ring   Button

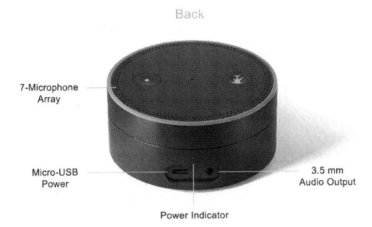

Back

7-Microphone
Array

Micro-USB   3.5 mm
Power   Audio Output

Power Indicator

The Echo Dot Can Utilize External Speakers

The Echo Dot, although its speakers aren't as strong as the original Echo, becomes a force to be reckoned with once it is connected to an external speaker. Connecting a 3.5mm audio cord from the Amazon Echo Dot to an external speaker can accomplish this task. This allows all of the sound traveling from your Echo Dot to now project from your external speaker.

In order to use your Echo Dot properly when connected to an external speaker, ensure that your Dot is a proper distance away from the speaker. This distance is usually 3 feet. Also make certain that your Amazon Echo Dot is more than 8 inches away from walls or any other devices or objects.

The Echo Dot and the Voice Remote for the Amazon Echo

Much like the previous version of the Echo Dot and the Echo, the second generation Echo Dot is compatible with the Voice Remote for the Amazon Echo. The Voice Remote connects to the Echo Dot via Bluetooth technology.

The Voice Remote is used as an optional addition to your Alexa-enabled devices, which can be utilized to speak to each of them. However, only one remote can be paired to one Echo device at a time.

The Alexa app will be used in order to enable your remote to work with your Echo Dot. From your Alexa application, open your left navigation and select *Settings*. From here, select the device that you want to connect with the remote. Select *Pair Device Remote* in order to proceed and to pair your remote with the selected device.

Long press the "Play" button on your remote for approximately 5 seconds in order to begin pairing with your device. It generally takes 40 seconds or longer to find and pair the device. Once the setup is complete, you will receive a message from Alexa saying "Your remote has been paired."

The Echo Dot and Alexa Skills

Since the Echo Dot is a part of the Alexa family, it is able to take full advantage of all the skills that the Alexa app has to offer. Alexa, in conjunction with the Amazon Echo Dot, acts as a virtual assistant to your everyday needs.

Being that the Echo Dot can do everything the original Echo can, it has no shortage of functionality. Alexa offers a wide range of skills, the most advertised being:

- Capital One

- Uber

- 1-800-Flowers

- Domino's

- Lyft

- StubHub

Alexa skills aid users in customizing the Echo Dot to their own personal needs. These skills help you in adding further functionality to your Echo Dot. Skills can be added through the Alexa app by simply selecting *Skills* from the left navigation panel.

The Alexa Family

Being that the Echo Dot is a part of the Alexa family, it is necessary to see how it stacks up against its siblings. Other Amazon Alexa-enabled devices include the original Amazon Echo, the first generation Echo Dot, and the Amazon Tap.

The Tap, Dot, and Echo have numerous similarities; however, there are also stark differences with each product. Each product is aimed at a different type of user with different needs.

The Amazon Tap is Amazon's portable Alexa device. One of the major differences of this device is that it is not "always on." Simply saying "Alexa" will not wake this device. Instead, the microphone (talk) button on the front of the Tap must be pressed. The microphone button is also not the only button on this device. The minimalist designs of the Echo and the Echo Dot have been slightly altered on the Tap to fit a more portable lifestyle.

There are buttons for the Wi-Fi and Bluetooth, dedicated playback buttons, and a power button. It also does not encompass the traditional ring lighting, but rather four indicator lights on the front. The one major difference is the battery. The Echo and the Echo Dot both operate on power adapters whereas the Tap has a non-removable, rechargeable battery. The Tap also comes with a charging cradle and power adapter for said cradle. It is also the only device to come with Dolby audio.

The Amazon Echo is the original and larger form of the Echo Dot. It houses a mono speaker. Unlike the four buttons on the Echo Dot, the Echo has two buttons: the action button and mute button. However, the Bluetooth audio output, AUX audio input/output are also not a part of the Echo. When playing music, the Echo gives a strong, rich sound unlike the other two devices. The Echo Dot and the Echo hold a number of similarities and are essentially able to perform the same functions.

The Amazon Echo Dot is the smaller form of the Echo and can perform all of the same Alexa functions. The sound quality of the Amazon Echo Dot is not as strong as the Echo but this can be compensated by connecting it to an external speaker. The Echo Dot also has some functions that the Echo does not have. These include having an AUX audio output and Bluetooth audio output.

Music and Media with Your Amazon Echo

The Amazon Echo Dot boasts a variety of avenues to listen to not only music but books as well. Its connection with third-party applications and subscription services makes it appealing to a variety of users.

However, even for the user who does not hold a music subscription, they are still able to connect the Dot to their library using Alexa.

Listening to Music on Your Alexa Device

Your Echo Dot can be used to stream music, listen to podcasts, audiobooks, and so much more. Your music library can also be added to your music library on Amazon from iTunes, Google Play, and many others.

Alexa can also be asked to stream music from various subscription services. These services include free and paid music subscriptions.

These subscription services consist of the following:

- Amazon Music

- Spotify Premium

- TuneIn

- Audible

- iHeartRadio

- Prime Music

- Amazon Music Unlimited

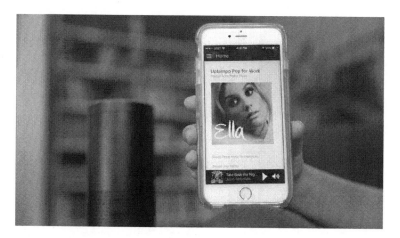

Upload Music to Your Library

In order to play your personal music library, Amazon Music for PC or Mac must be used in order to upload into the "My Music" section on Amazon. 250 songs can be uploaded for free; however, in order to add more songs you must have an Amazon Music Subscription.

Note: Tracks purchased via the Digital Music Store do not go towards the 250 song limit on free accounts.

Third-Party Music Services

In order to successfully listen to third-party music services, you will be required to link your music service account within Alexa. This can be done by easily selecting *Music & Books* from the navigation panel within the app and selecting the desired streaming service. After selecting your desired streaming service, select *Link Account to Alexa* and sign in with your respective credentials. You will now be able to use Alexa in combination with your desired service.

Audible and Kindle Unlimited

Audible and Kindle can also be used with the Echo Dot in order to stream audiobooks and other media. This may include newspaper and magazine audio subscriptions, statistics, notes, bookmarks, and narration speed controls.

LENDING LIBRARY

Sample commands include:

- *"Play the book, [Huckleberry Finn]."*

- *"Stop reading the book in [60] minutes."*

- *"Play [title of work] from Audible."*

Alexa also has the ability to read items from Amazon Kindle. Eligible books include items that have been purchased from the Kindle store, items shared within your Family Library, or items borrowed from Kindle Unlimited or Kindle Owners' Lending Library.

Alexa is currently not able to support comics, graphic novels, or narration speed control. Sample commands to Alexa for Amazon Kindle may include:

- *"Read my Kindle Book."*

- *"Read my book, [book title]."*

Music Unlimited for Echo Devices

The Amazon Music subscription allows you access to a diverse range of music on your Echo Dot device. Using Alexa and your Echo Dot you are able to purchase your Amazon Music Unlimited for Echo Subscription. If your associated account has never purchased a music subscription, you will be eligible to purchase the free trial via voice commands.

Note: The free trial places a $1 hold on your account that will be removed within 72 hours.

In order to complete the process of signing up for a music subscription via Alexa, simply say "Sign up for Amazon Music Unlimited." Alexa will then guide you through the needed steps.

News, Weather, and Traffic

Your Echo Dot is more than just a speaker to play and listen to music. Your Alexa-enabled Dot is able to provide updates on the latest news headlines through the use of flash briefings, sports updates, weather data, and even movie information.

Alexa on your Dot is also smart enough to provide answers to questions related to simple trivia, history, and a variety of other categories. Supplying you with address and telephone information for various businesses is another Alexa-enabled task.

Flash Briefings

Your flash briefing is a way to receive updates from popular broadcasters, weather information, and the latest headlines from the Associated Press.

You can customize your settings for your Flash Briefings within the Alexa app. Things that are customizable are: shows, various headlines, and weather updates. You can also edit the order in which the programs play in your flash briefings.

Using the "Get More Flash Briefing Content" skill gives you the ability to view more flash briefing content. Once the flash brief is read by Alexa a link will appear in your Alexa application in order for you to read the full stories.

Sample commands for your Flash Briefing include the following:

- *"What's my flash briefing?"*

- *"What's new?"*

Sports Updates

Alexa is able to give information about the latest scores and game information for your favorite teams. However, these teams must first be set up in the Alexa app before this feature can be used.

In order to add your sports teams from the Alexa app select **Settings > Sports Update.** Enter the name of your desired sports team into the search field. Suggestions appear as you enter your team name.

In order to hear your sports updates simply tell Alexa *"Give me my Sports Update."*

Check Your Weather

Your Echo Dot can also give you your local weather forecast as well as the weather in any international or U.S city. Adding your address in the Alexa app can also be done in order to ensure your weather is more accurate. Editing your device location from the Alexa settings menu option can easily change your location.

Within the Alexa app a seven-day forecast will appear when asking Alexa about the weather. AccuWeather is used by Alexa in order to obtain the latest weather information.

Sample commands to be used with the weather include:

- *"What's the weather?"*

- *"What's the weather for this weekend?"*

- *"Will it rain tomorrow?"*

Traffic Requests

Setting up traffic updates in Alexa is easy; however, you must first have a travel route set within the app. The starting location is usually set to the address you have associated with your Amazon account.

Alexa can update you on traffic conditions along your desired route, the duration of your route, and provide the quickest route options. From your Alexa app select **Settings > Traffic**. Update the "from" and "to" address.

In order to get traffic updates from Alexa simply ask "*How is traffic?*" or "*What's my commute?*"

Nearby Locations

The Amazon Echo Dot also allows you to find local restaurants, various businesses, and shops near your current address. In order to find places nearby Alexa uses your device location in combination with Yelp.

With Alexa, you are able to search by different areas in order to find exactly what you are looking for. These search terms include searching for different business types, searching for top-rated businesses, or getting the address of a nearby business. Alexa also provides business hours and phone numbers.

Finding Movie Showtimes

Your Echo Dot can also aid you in finding movies and movie showtimes. You don't even have to grab your cell phone! Once your address is set up in the Alexa app you will be able to find what movies are playing near you. Alexa uses IMDb to find specific theaters and movies.

Using your Dot you are able to find out what movies are playing near you, movies playing in other cities as well as specific showtimes. You can also be more specific with your requests by asking to find specific showtimes at a specific theater.

Ask Alexa

Your Echo Dot can answer a variety of questions related to people, places, dates, history, trivia, and many others. Alexa can also spell and define words as well as do simple calculations.

Sample Alexa commands may include:

- *"When is [holiday]?"*

- *"Who is [person name]?"*

- *"Who starred in the TV Show [title]?"*

- *"Who starred in the Movie [title]?"*

Productivity

The Echo Dot is an amazing tool for the individual who is constantly planning, using to-do lists, and updating their calendars. Alexa on your Dot has the ability to not only wake you up when needed, but it also gives you updates on various tasks and events.

Timers and Alarms

Alexa can be used to set multiple timers or alarms as needed. Timers and alarms can be set up to 24 hours ahead of time.

After creating alarms with your voice you can edit them inside of the Alexa app. You can also create new alarms, as well as turn them on or off from within the Alexa app.

Changing your alarm volume, alarm sound, or deleting an alarm are three functionalities that must be performed from within the Alexa app.

Sample voice commands for alarms include:

- *"What time is my alarm set for today?"*

- *"What repeating alarms do I have?"*

- *"Set a repeating alarm for [day of week] at [time]."*

- *"Wake me up at [time]."*

Timers offer a different variety of functionality. However, pausing or resuming your timer and changing the timer volume can only be done through the Alexa app.

Note: A timer's volume cannot be altered using the device volume; they are independent of one another.

Sample voice commands that can be used with timers include:

- *"Set a timer for [x amount of time]."*

- *"Set the timer for [time]."*

Manage Lists

Lists can be used with your Amazon Echo Dot in order to keep track of important tasks. Each list item can be a maximum list of 256 characters with 100 items on each list.

Your lists (shopping lists and to-do lists) can be accessed from the Alexa app, the Amazon app, and the Alexa Shopping list. There is also the option to link third-party list services to Alexa.

Using your Echo Dot, Alexa is able to add an item to your shopping or to-do list and review the items on your list.

Linking Third-Party List Services to Your Echo Dot

When your Echo Dot is used with third-party list services it provides a way for you to better manage tasks and things you want to remember.

To link a service in the Alexa app, navigate to your *Settings > Lists* and select *Link* for the desired list service. Enter in your login information or create a new account. Use the on screen prompts to complete setup.

Adding or Reviewing Calendar Events

The Dot can be used with Alexa in order to add or review events in your Google Calendar. In order to start using the calendar features

within Alexa you must first link your Google Calendar within the Alexa app.

To do so, navigate to **Settings** > **Calendar** and select **Google Calendar**. Select **Link Google Calendar Account** in order to link your active Google calendar.

Before you can begin to add events to your calendar you must first ensure that the proper calendar is selected for the events to be added to it.

Sample commands for utilizing the calendar include:

- *"When is my next event?"*

- *"What's on my calendar on [day]?"*

- *"Add [event] to my calendar for [day] at [time]."*

Using Voicecast to Send Content

Your Echo Dot can also serve as a way for sending details about news, weather, and various other areas to your Fire tablet. Turning on Automatic Voicecast allows you to send content automatically to your Fire tablet.

When content is sent to your Fire tablet it will appear on the lock screen of the tablet. When the device is unlocked, a notification appears in the Quick Settings menu on the Fire tablet.

Voicecast works with numerous amount of Alexa features including the following:

- Music

- Wikipedia

- Questions and answers

- Flash Briefing

- Lists

- Weather

- Timer and alarms

- Help

In order to send Alexa a request simply say *"Show this on my Fire tablet"* or *"Send that to [device name]."*

IFTTT

The Echo Dot supports use with IFTTT also known as "If This, Then That." IFTTT is a third-party service that automates how apps, websites, and other devices operate with each other.

The Amazon Alexa channel on If This, Then That allows users to cycle through a list of predefined recipes that will work with your Echo device. These incorporate some common tasks that work with the Dot and various other Alexa products.

In order to get started with using IFTTT and your Dot you must first link your IFTTT account with the Alexa app. Once this is complete you will be able to set up actions, recipes, etc.

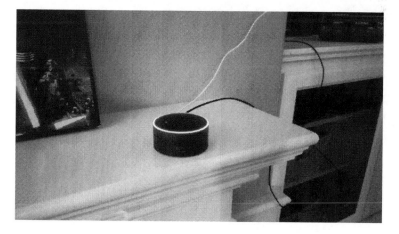

Shopping

The Echo Dot also allows you to do particular shopping from your device. You have the ability to buy music, order an Alexa device, or place orders using Alexa.

Placing Orders with Alexa

When making a purchase using your Echo Dot, Alexa has the ability to search through various purchase options. These purchase option searches include:

- Your order history: Only Prime-eligible items are available to be ordered using Alexa.

- Prime-eligible items: These items include items that are eligible for delivery by Prime Now.

- Amazon's Choice: These items are high-rated and well-priced products with Prime shipping

When attempting to purchase an item through Alexa, she will always tell you the item name and price before purchasing. She is also able to provide additional shipping information if it will not be delivered through Amazon Prime. After providing all of the needed information Alexa will have you either confirm or cancel the order.

Alexa will also give you the option to add items to your cart on Amazon, add items to an Alexa Shopping list, or refer to the application for more information. These options will only be provided in the event that your requested item can't be found or the purchase could not be completed.

In order to place an order using your Alexa device certain requirements must also be set up on your Amazon account.

In order to place an order from the Digital Music Store you must have an annual Prime Membership, an Amazon account and a payment method set up in 1-click settings. The same requirements apply for ordering physical products.

Shopping settings can be managed through the Alexa app. You have the option to turn off voice purchasing as well as require a confirmation code before every order.

In order to purchase Prime-eligible items, with a quantity no greater than twelve for each item, the following commands may be used:

- *"Order a [item name]."* A response of yes/no is needed once Alexa has found the product in order to confirm.

- *"Reorder [item name]."* A response of yes/no is needed once Alexa has found the product in order to confirm.

- *"Add [item name] to my cart."* This will add an item to your cart on Amazon.

- *"Cancel my order."* This function will cancel an order immediately after placing it.

When purchasing music, if desired, a confirmation code may also be used before initiating a purchase. This stops anyone from being able to purchase music on your account. To buy music using Alexa, the following commands may be used:

- *"Shop for the song [song name]."*

- *"Shop for the album [album name]."*

- *"Buy this [song]."* This command can be used when a song is currently playing on an Amazon-supported station.

Tracking Orders with Your Echo Dot

Your Echo Dot also allows you to track orders via Alexa. If you have more than one open order, Alexa will provide the status of the order with a delivery date closest to the current date.

Simply asking Alexa, *"Where is my stuff?"* or *"Track my order"* will prompt Alexa for order information.

Aside from all of these things that your Amazon Echo Dot can do, it

is also able to serve as a hub for your home control. The Echo Dot is able to control your lights, various switches around your home, your thermostat, and also items like Phillips, Hive, or Hue devices. There are a variety of devices available for purchase with the Amazon Echo Dot all of which are outlined in the next chapter.

Chapter 2: The Echo Dot and Wi-Fi

Connecting Your Echo Dot to Your Home Wi-Fi Network

If you haven't already, plug your Echo Dot into a wall socket and open the Alexa app.

One irritating bug on the new Dot, which wasn't a problem with the old one, is that it does not recognize the Verizon Fios 5GHz network router, even though both generations lay claim to supporting dual band Wi-Fi on 2.4 and 5GHz bands on networks that use the 802.11a/b/g/n standard. The new Dot did, however, recognize the Verizon router's 2.4GHz band, and also the 5GHz band on other routers. The Echo Dot does not connect to ad-hoc (or peer-to-peer) networks.

1. Open the left navigation panel in the Alexa app and choose *Settings*.

2. Select **Setup a New Device** to add your new Echo Dot.
3. Press and hold the **Action** button on your Echo device for five seconds. When the light ring around the top of the Echo device changes to orange, then your mobile device can connect to your Echo device. A list of available networks should appear.
4. Select your Wi-Fi network and enter the network password (if required). If your Wi-Fi network isn't listed, scroll down and select **Add a Network** (for hidden networks) or **Rescan**.

    MAC address: If you need to add your Alexa device to your router's list of approved devices, scroll down on that screen until you see the MAC address.

    Optional: Save your Wi-Fi password to Amazon: Any Wi-Fi passwords saved during setup automatically appear when you connect a new Alexa device to the same Wi-Fi network. The password is also remembered if you switch between saved Wi-Fi networks.

    Optional: Connect to a public network: Enter any required information if you are connecting to a public network that requires a web browser to sign in, like a school or hotel. The information could be a pre-shared password, room number, or just a button to accept conditions for using the network. This information cannot be saved to Amazon. Contact the network owner for more information.

5. Select **Connect**. After your device connects to your Wi-Fi network, a confirmation message appears in the app. You're now ready to use Alexa.

Your Echo Device Doesn't Connect to the Wi-Fi Network.

Make sure your Wi-Fi network meets the standards of dual-band Wi-Fi (2.4 GHz/5 GHz) networks that use the 802.11a/b/g/n.

The power LED on your Echo device shows the current status of your Wi-Fi network. You can locate the power LED near the power adapter port on the device.

Power LED State	Description
Solid white light	Your Echo device is connected to your Wi-Fi network.
Solid orange light	Your Echo device is not connected to your Wi-Fi network.
Blinking orange light	Your Echo device is connected to your Wi-Fi network, but can't access the Alexa Voice Service.

➢ Try to connect to the Wi-Fi network again.
➢ Make sure you know your network password (if required). If you see a lock icon, a network password is required. This password is not your Amazon account password.
➢ Verify if other devices (such as tablets or mobile phones) can connect to your network. If not, there may be a problem with your Wi-Fi network. You should contact your Internet service provider, network administrator, or the person who set up your network for assistance.
➢ Update the firmware for your router or modem hardware.
➢ If you saved your Wi-Fi password to Amazon, but you recently changed the password, you need to re-enter your new Wi-Fi password to connect again.

> By default, your router may use both WPA+WPA2 for security. To resolve connection issues, switch the router security type to either WPA or WPA2 only. If the router also has an option to set the type of encryption, setting it to AES only is recommended.

Reduce Wi-Fi Congestion

> If you have multiple devices on your Wi-Fi network, you may have inconsistent Wi-Fi performance.
> Turn off devices you aren't using to free up bandwidth on your network.
> Move your device closer to your router and modem if it's in a different room or blocked by an object.
> Make sure your device is away from sources of possible interference, such as microwave ovens or baby monitors.
> **Optional:** Connect to your router's 5 GHz Wi-Fi frequency band (if it's available). Many Wi-Fi devices only connect to the 2.4 GHz band. If multiple devices use this band on your network, your network speed may be slower. You can connect to the less congested 5 GHz band for better range and less interference.

Restart Your Echo Device and Network Hardware

➤ You can restart your Echo device, Internet modem, and/or router to resolve most intermittent Wi-Fi issues.

➤ Turn off your router and modem, and then wait 30 seconds.

➤ Turn on your modem, and then wait for it to restart.

➤ After you restart your modem, turn on your router, and then wait for it to restart.

➤ While your network hardware restarts, unplug the power adapter from your Echo device for three seconds, and then plug it back in.

➤ After you restart your Echo device and network hardware, try to connect to your Wi-Fi network again.

If you still can't connect, you may want to contact your Internet service provider, your router manufacturer, or your network administrator.

There is one caution that you should be aware of when setting up your Echo Dot initially. You may or may not have already set up an Amazon Echo, but if so, you should remember this: there is a step in the process, in the Alexa app, that requires you to disconnect your phone or tablet from your home/personal Wi-Fi network and connect to the Dot as your wireless router. Of course, before doing so, you will need to connect your Echo Dot to your Wi-Fi network so that your phone or tablet can find the Dot in the network device list.

Simple to Set Up & Use

1. Plug in Echo Dot

2. Connect to the internet with the Alexa App

3. Just ask for music, weather, news, and more

Alexa App is available for Android, iOS, and Fire devices

Connecting to a Wi-Fi Hotspot

You can connect your Echo Dot to a Wi-Fi hotspot on your mobile device if you're not near your home or a public Wi-Fi network. But before you do, please note:

- ✓ You will need the latest software update (3389 or higher) for your Echo Dot. The most recent version for your Echo or Echo Dot (First Generation) is 4148; Echo Dot (Second Generation) is 5.5.0.1. This is the update that downloads and installs the latest ESP (Echo Spatial Perception) technology that helps your devices better understand which one should answer your question or request.
- ✓ You will need a cellular service plan that supports Wi-Fi hotspots
- ✓ You will need the Alexa app on a supported mobile device (iOS, Android)

Do you have the most recent software version?

Note: The option to connect your Dot to a mobile hotspot may not be available when you set it up for the first time. If it isn't, you will need to connect your Echo Dot to your home Wi-Fi network to download and install the most recent software update which enables this feature. Alexa updates are automatically downloaded when connected to a Wi-Fi network. You always want the latest updates because they typically fix issues from previous updates and improve performance and add new Alexa features.

You determine the current software version of your Alexa devices in the Alexa app by opening the left navigation panel and selecting *Settings*. Highlight your device and then scroll down until you see ***Device Software Version***.

If you do not have the latest version (as noted in bullets above) make sure your device is on and has an active Wi-Fi connection. You should avoid saying anything to your device while the update is running. The light ring on your device turns blue when it is ready to install. Depending on the speed of your Wi-Fi network, it could take up to 15 minutes for the install to complete.

Note: If you are experiencing issues with the software update downloading, it's best to restart your device to see if this corrects the issue. You restart the Echo devices by unplugging the power adaptor from the back of the device and then plugging it back in. After restarting your device, wait for the update to install again.

Connecting Your Echo Dot to a Wi-Fi Hotspot:

1. In the *Settings* menu, on your mobile device, search for a Wi-Fi hotspot option and copy the network name and password for your hotspot.
2. Open the left navigation panel in the Alexa app and select *Settings*.
3. Locate and select your Echo Dot device and then select *Update Wi-Fi*.
4. Press and hold the *Action* button on your Echo Dot for five seconds. When the light ring around the top of the device turns orange, your mobile device connects to your Echo Dot and a list of available Wi-Fi networks appears.

   Note: Alexa may ask you to manually connect your device to your Echo Dot through your Wi-Fi settings.
5. Scroll down and select *Use this device as a Wi-Fi hotspot*.
6. Select *Start*.
7. Enter the Wi-Fi hotspot network name and password that you copied from the *Settings* menu on your mobile device. If unable to paste the information, be sure to enter the network information exactly as it is displayed on your mobile device or your Echo Dot won't be able to connect to your Wi-Fi hotspot.
8. Go to your mobile device's *Settings* menu and turn on your Wi-Fi hotspot. Your Echo Dot will search for your Wi-Fi hotspot and connect. Alexa will confirm a successful connection.

Important: When using your mobile device as a Wi-Fi hotspot your Echo Dot uses the device's data connection. Additional charges may be applied from your service provider depending on your current data plan. Contact your service provider with any questions you may have about data usage when your Echo Dot is connected to your Wi-Fi hotspot.

Chapter 3: The Echo/Echo Dot Voice Remote

The official remote for the Echo and Echo Dot connects to the devices via Bluetooth. The size of the remote is 5.5 inches long and 1.5 inches wide. The integrated microphone in the remote can be used when you are too far away from Alexa or the room is too noisy for her to hear you. You can use the remote from any room in your house and its capable distance is up to 100+ feet away. The remote has buttons for moving to the next or previous track, playing or pausing, and controlling the volume when you use it to control the device(s). The remote works with only one Echo device at a time and is not compatible with the Amazon Tap or the Fire TV.

This remote is shipped with 2 AAA batteries to get you started with the setup right out of the box. However, when the batteries need to be changed, you may find it difficult to remove the battery cover to replace them. The best way to do this is to hold the remote face down in the palm of your hand with the top pointed away from you. Find the battery cover tab, indicated by what appears to be the inside of an equal sign, and using something hard, yet not sharp, press down on the tab while also pulling the bottom of the cover up. Be sure you aren't gripping the remote in a way that blocks the cover from coming off. It's a little tricky but not that difficult.

If the remote instructions are not included you can get the instructions from the Alexa app in the **Settings** menu option. Just select **Pair device remote** and the device that you want to pair it with will ask you to press and hold the play button on the remote for a few seconds until it's been discovered. Once it's discovered you are ready to use it.

To activate the voice control you will need to press and hold the mic button while you speak. This means you don't have to use your chosen wake word (Alexa, Amazon, or Echo) with the remote. For example, while pushing/holding the mic button, just say your command "*Turn on office*" and depending on the skill you've setup, the office lights, etc. will be turned on. Be aware that you will need to hold the mic button for the whole command to be heard and understood. You cannot just press and release while speaking.

As stated above, the remote can only be used on one device at a time. However, if you wish to pair a second remote, so you can have one in different parts of the house, you can do so by going to the Alexa app and choosing **Settings > Echo > Bluetooth > Pair a new device.** Once the pair process begins, press the play button on the second remote for about 5 seconds until it is shown as an *Unknown Device* in the device list. When you connect to it the Echo it looks like it is pairing another Bluetooth speaker, but it is actually the second remote. The second remote will not show up anywhere in the Bluetooth device list but both remotes will then work with that Echo device. This means you can use two remotes with one Echo device or pair each remote with its own Echo device.

When Alexa finds it difficult to hear or understand you due to noise or loud volume, you can also use the remote to pause or stop the music or loud volume, and then use the device to control Alexa by speaking to it once it is quiet enough.

One disappointing fact with the remote is that it came as a package deal with the first generation Echo and Echo Dot for Amazon Prime members, but it is not packaged with the second generation Echo Dot. Also, when purchased as a package the remote came with a magnetic holster. The holster is no longer included when purchased separately, which is now required.

Chapter 4: Fun Functions and Advanced Settings

Functions, Fun, and Advanced Settings on Your Echo Dot

Knowing the basics of interaction with all of the different features of Amazon Echo Dot, here are some of the functions that Echo Dot can do. The following will touch on some of the fun little quirks it has and talk about some advanced settings the device also has.

To-Do and Shopping Lists

The Alexa app has a to-do list and a shopping list section that can be populated by talking to Echo Dot. Add an item to your to-do list by saying a phrase like "*Alexa, put [action] on my to-do list.*" Add an item to a shopping list by saying something like "*Alexa, add [item] to my shopping list.*" For a complete list of phrases that you can use to add tasks and items to your to-do and shopping lists, see Amazon's updated phrasing list located in the Amazon user help files.

Alarms and Timers

Echo Dot supports setting timers and alarms. To set timers, say something like *"Set a timer for 45 minutes."* The timer for 45 minutes starts as soon as Alexa confirms the timer has been set and there is no delay when the timer starts. Dot supports advanced alarms, which is not how the Echo operated originally before receiving software updates. Setting both one-off and repeating alarms is supported by Alexa, so it can be used for waking up every morning at a certain time and setting reminders about unique tasks. To set an alarm for, 6:26 a.m. today, just say *"Set an alarm for 6:26 this morning."* To set an alarm for every evening at 8:00, say *"Set an alarm for 8:00 in the evening every day."*

Recall that timers and alarms that have been set can be viewed in the Alexa app.

Changing the Wake Word

Echo Dot comes preset to recognize the word "Alexa" as the wake word. Dot knows if you're talking to it or not when the wake word is used. The wake word can be changed to the word "Amazon" by using the Alexa app. To make this change, open the Alexa app, swipe open and look at the left-hand menu, open the **Settings** section, tap on the Echo Dot in the device list. Select the **Wake word option**, and there it can be changed between the words "Alexa" and "Amazon." When changing the wake word for Dot, the device may standby for a few moments while it reconfigures to recognize the new word.

Reset to Factory Defaults

For a user having trouble getting Echo Dot to listen or perform as it should, try resetting it. There are intermittent issues with any device from time to time, and though they usually work out within a short time, there have been some occasions where the device needs to be fully reset to get it to work properly. To reset Echo Dot, use a paperclip, turn the Echo Dot upside down and insert the paperclip into the small hole that is labeled RESET to press the reset button. Hold the button for 10–20 seconds. The light ring will turn on, turn off, and then turn on again before beginning the setup of Echo Dot like when it was first received.

Fun Phrases to Try Out

Below is a partial list of fun and entertaining phrases for Echo Dot, or any device that has Alexa. This list is not complete; the Amazon Alexa development team has put many more than these into Alexa.

Alexa, I am your father.

Alexa, who lives in a pineapple under the sea?

Alexa, what is the loneliest number?

Alexa, how many roads must a man walk down?

Alexa, all your base are belong to us.

Alexa, how much is that doggie in the window?

Alexa, Romeo, Romeo wherefore art thou Romeo?

Alexa, define rock, paper, scissors, lizard, Spock.

Alexa, beam me up.

Alexa, how much wood can a woodchuck chuck if a woodchuck could chuck wood?

Alexa, define supercalifragilisticexpialodocious.

Alexa, who's your daddy?

Alexa, Earl Grey. Hot. (or Alexa, tea. Earl Grey. Hot.)

Alexa, what is the meaning of life?

Alexa, what does the Earth weigh?

Alexa, when is the end of the world?

Alexa, is there a Santa?

Alexa, make me a sandwich.

Alexa, what is the best tablet?

Alexa, what is your favorite color?

Alexa, who won best actor Oscar in 1973?

Alexa, what is your quest?

Alexa, what is the airspeed velocity of an unladen swallow?

Alexa, where do babies come from?

Alexa, do you have a boyfriend?

Alexa, which comes first: the chicken or the egg?

Alexa, may the force be with you.

Alexa, do aliens exist?

Alexa, how many licks does it take to get to the center of a Tootsie pop?

Alexa, what are you going to do today?

Alexa, where do you live?

Alexa, do you want to build a snowman?

Alexa, do you really want to hurt me?

Alexa, what is love?

Alexa, who is the real Slim Shady?

Alexa, who let the dogs out?

Alexa, open the pod bay doors.

Troubleshooting

In the majority of cases where Dot freezes up or refuses to listen to voice commands, the issue can be solved by unplugging then re-plugging the device back in again. Sometimes the unit may not be working due to a software update, or because the Internet connection was interrupted. Echo operates by sending a question or phrase spoken to it to Amazon's servers, which interpret the command and tell it how to respond based on that information. In a few cases, restarting the Echo may not fix it. Alternatively try to leave it unplugged for a few hours and plug it back in; some users have reported that doing so solved the issue. It is highly likely that this is because of another unrelated issue, like software updates or issues communicating with the Amazon servers. If Echo Dot continues to perform poorly or not at all, refer to the previous section that describes how to perform a factory reset. It will have to be set up again on an Amazon account and Wi-Fi network if you reset. In a majority of cases it will fix the problem. When nothing else is working do not forget to contact Amazon's customer support through their website. The customer service team at Amazon is phenomenal, and they can assist with a repair or replacement if the user has already tried resetting and restarting Dot.

Chapter 5: Using Your Amazon Echo Dot (Second Generation) as a Smart Home

The Amazon Echo Dot is truly a little powerhouse that is made for any room. Place your Dot in the bedroom for a quick alarm clock or in the living room when you are just looking to hear some tunes. The Amazon Dot is capable of working with a number of varying devices for the purpose of making your home smarter and more efficient. The Echo Dot is the perfect tool to begin the Home Automation Process. These smart options can be purchased with the Dot from Amazon.com.

Using Your Amazon Dot with the Bose Soundlink Mini II

The Amazon Echo Dot can be easily used with a wide variety of Bluetooth speakers. The Bose Soundlink Mini II is just one option for pairing with the device. On a full charge the Bose Soundlink Mini II can play up for up to 10 hours. Voice prompts on the device will walk you through the Bluetooth connection process.

Connect your Dot via Bluetooth or through the 3.5mm stereo cable. To pair via Bluetooth follow the following instructions:

1. Place your Bose Soundlink Mini II in pairing mode.

2. On your phone or tablet, select **Settings** within the Alexa app.

3. Your Dot will enter pairing mode after selecting **Bluetooth > Pair a New Device**. Your Bose speaker will appear in the list of devices once it is found. Select your speaker.

4. Once your speaker has successfully connected, Alexa will give you confirmation. From then on you can connect and disconnect from your speaker simply using your voice.

Using Your Amazon Dot with the Phillips Hue Starter Kit

Make controlling your home lighting a cinch when you pair the Amazon Dot with the Phillips Hue Starter kit. Although the starter kit only comes with a bridge and two bulbs, the bridge can wirelessly connect to up to 50 lights. The two included bulbs offered in this kit are 800 lumens, a step up from the first generation kit where the bulbs were only 600 lumens.

The bridge also allows you to control lighting from your device or even from your Amazon Dot Echo using Alexa. Setting up your Phillips lighting with Alexa is fairly easy and can be done quickly.

1. On your smart device open the Alexa app and navigate to **Settings**.

2. From Settings open **Connected Home** in the account section. From there, choose **Discover Devices** in the device section.

3. At this time, press the button on your Phillips Hue Bridge in order to enable connection. Your bulbs should appear in the devices section. Within this section you have the ability to create groups which represent specific rooms in order to control a complete room of lights. Your lights are now ready to use.

Note: In order to do more than brighten and dim your lights you will need to authorize Alexa to work with your IFTTT (If This, Then That) account. Once this is complete you can create triggers and specific phrases to control lighting functions.

Using Your Amazon Dot with the TP-Link Smart Plug

The TP-Link Smart plug is another way you can use Alexa to control your home. The smart plug allows you to control your device from any location using the TP-Link Kasa App, schedule the automation of electronics as needed, and utilize "Away Mode." Away Mode allows you to turn your devices on and off at various times in order to give the illusion that you are at home when you are away.

The TP-Link can be used to not only control lighting but to also control the television or whatever device is plugged into it. Like most setup with the Amazon Echo Dot, it is easy. Follow the instructions below in order to ensure your TP- Link Smart Plug is set up properly.

1. From the Alexa app, select **Smart Home**. Since this is a new setup you will potentially need to add this skill to the Smart Home area. Simply search for **TP-Link Kasa**.

2. Once you have located the skill, simply select **Enable skill** and log into your TP-Link account.

3. In order for your device to work properly with the Amazon Echo Dot you must first turn on the **Remote Control** function from the Kasa app. You can do this by simply going into your desired device > Select the **Settings** icon > under **Device Controls**, select **Remote Control**.

4. Place Alexa in **Discover Mode** by simply saying "*Alexa discover devices.*" Your Dot should then discover your Smart Plug. Once discovery is complete you will now be able to control the desired device with your voice.

Using Your Amazon Dot with the ecobee3 Smart Thermostat

Ensure you never have to walk to the thermostat again when you purchase the Amazon Echo Dot in conjunction with the ecobee3 Smart Thermostat. The ecobee3 Smart Thermostat works to ensure that you are comfortable at all times. It has the ability to sense when rooms are occupied or when no one is home.

To connect your Dot to your ecobee3 follow the following instructions:

1. Open your Alexa app and navigate to the **Settings**.

2. From the settings select **Connected Home**. Once in this area scroll until you see **Device Links**. Select **Link with ecobee**.

3. You will then be asked to log into your ecobee account and authorize ecobee with your device.

4. It will then show **Unlink the ecobee** once the device has been successfully linked.

Linking these items with your Amazon Echo Dot (Second Generation) is only one way that it can be used. It offers a plethora of other functionality. Other featured brands which perform with the Amazon Echo Dot include:

- Samsung SmartThings

- WeMo

- Insteon

- Wink

- Honeywell

Smart Home Device Groups

Within the Alexa application you are able to create a device group which allows you to control multiple smart home devices all at once.

1. In order to create a smart home group, locate **Smart Home** from your left navigation panel in the Alexa app.

2. Select **Groups** > **Create Groups**.

3. Enter your desired group name. Room names are generally used to give your group a recognizable name.

4. Select the devices in which you would like to add to this group. Select **Add** once you are complete.

Once your group has been created in the Alexa app you are now able to use commands via Alexa with it. For some skills you may need to tell Alexa to "*Open [skill name]*" before your request can be recognized and completed. Sample commands to be used with your smart home devices may include the following:

- *"Turn on [Smart Device Name or group]."*

- *"Set [Group Name] to [#]%."*

- *"Set my living room fan to [#]%."*

Your device scene can be managed through the desired device's companion application. Scene names are shown in the Smart Home section of the Alexa application.

Chapter 6: Using IFTTT with Your Amazon Echo Dot

IFTTT allows you to connect various applications and create chains of conditional statements referred to as "Recipes." It essentially is an automation service for the majority of your things connected via the Internet.

IFTTT is a cellular application as well as a website that is used to automate everything from Smart Home items to simple notifications on your phone. It works extremely well with Phillips Hue systems, Alexa, and various other applications.

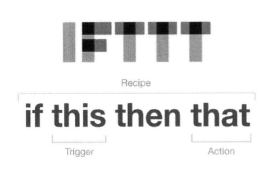

Use your IFTTT application with Alexa to setup recipes for use with the following applications:

- Phillips Hue

- Google Drive

- Todoist

- GMail

- Evernote

- Google Calendar

- Nest

- Harmony

Connecting the Echo Dot with IFTTT

IFTTT now has an Amazon Alexa Channel in which you can link your Echo Dot to various compatible functions.

In order to connect your Dot to IFTTT follow the instructions below.

1. Navigate to the Alexa Channel page from your IFTTT application. Select the **Connect** button in order to begin setup.

2. You will then be prompted to sign into your Amazon account, which is associated with your Echo Dot. You will also be prompted to share some additional information with

IFTTT. Select *I Agree* in order to move forward. Your account will now be connected with Amazon.

3. From there you will see a list of predefined recipes, which work with Alexa. Choose your desired function and select **Turn On**. From that point forward anytime the associated action is performed, IFTTT will perform your selected action.

4. When selecting a pre-defined recipe, you have the option to configure that recipe or leave it as is. Ensure that you are reading the configuration in order to know how to trigger events with Alexa.

On each of your selected actions you will be shown the last time the trigger was ran and given the option to "check now" to determine if the trigger is working.

The Echo Dot, IFTTT and Your Smart Home

IFTTT is a central hub for creating and using recipes to run your smart home with. IFTTT and Alexa work extremely well with applications like SmartThings, Phillips Hue, and Harmony.

IFTTT allows Alexa to perform actions like changing the light color, toggling device power, locking doors, and turning lights on.

New recipes can also be created via the IFTTT dashboard by selecting the **Create New Recipe** link or to search for the application in which you choose to connect the recipe to.

1. After selecting the action or the application, proceed to choose a trigger from the variety selected.

2. Next you will need to complete the trigger field.

3. Choose your action channel. For example, if you are connecting light bulbs select the action channel for the product.

4. Choose an action associated to it. In the case of a light bulb the action can be "turn lights on," "turn lights off," or various other options. In the case of lighting there will be various other options like fading in, color options, etc.

5. Your trigger will then be available for use.

Chapter 7: Overcoming the Disadvantages of the Dot

Like any good item there will always be pros and cons. Although the Amazon Echo Dot (Second Generation) is a mighty powerhouse in a small package, the drop in size doesn't come without some sacrifices.

Below find the common issues with the Amazon Echo Dot and how to fix them.

- Dot Responsiveness

One complaint with the Amazon Echo Dot has been its lack of responsiveness or the proximity to which you have to be with your Dot in order for it to pick up your voice.

One way to fix this issue would be to re-run your voice training. If this has never been ran this is a good indicator as to why the Dot is not properly picking up your speech pattern or voice. To run the voice training simply follow the steps below:

1. Navigate to the Alexa app from your smart device.

2. Within the Alexa app select *Settings* > *Voice Training*.

3. Make sure you select the proper device from the top dropdown. This will be the device the voice training will be run on.

4. After selecting *Next* you will be prompted to read aloud through 25 phrases. Be sure to not only speak in your normal tone but also stand or sit your typical communication distance away from the device. If you complete your training with your voice right into or above the Dot it will rightfully not awaken when you are across the room.

- Sound Quality

Another slight disadvantage for some Dot users is the speaker. This issue may be more prevalent for users who have owned and used the full size Amazon Echo. Being that this is a smaller device, we cannot expect the same loud boisterous sound from this small device which comes from the larger Echo. Although not having a speaker connected to the Dot does not limit its functionality in any way, it may be helpful for the users who expect a bigger sound.

When the Dot is at full volume this can be considered half of the volume of the original Amazon Echo. It also lacks the richness of sound which the Amazon Echo encompasses. For this reason, the Echo Dot probably would not be your primary choice for a music speaker.

In order to bypass the Amazon Echo Dot speakers completely, connect an external speaker using the 3.5mm jack. This is one way to ensure that the internal speakers are disabled. However, please remember that if this is your intended functional path, your external speakers must always be turned on for communication with Alexa to occur.

- Unexpected Device Limitations

There are a number of activities that the Alexa app can perform with the Echo Dot device. You can ask questions, you can check your calendar and do a number of other things. However, in order for these things to work properly you must download the appropriate skills within the Alexa application.

All of the skills and features Alexa offers are located on the Alexa Help Page on Amazon.com. New features are being developed for Alexa and developers are making more apps to function with Alexa every day. Its functionality is continuously growing.

Even if you find that Alexa is missing something that you are looking for, within its wide range of functionality it is bound to be something that can perform a similar task. Before purchasing the Dot, or even directly after, it is always wise to see what Alexa offers and if it aligns to your needs in order to avoid unexpected limitations.

Being that Alexa works with IFTTT, this would allow your device to connect to a variety of applications that Alexa may not be directly compatible with alone.

- Issues with the Alexa App

The Alexa app is constantly being updated to make each of the Alexa compatible devices more responsive and smarter. If you receive an error message stating "The Alexa app is offline," there are a number of common solutions that will fix this.

1. **Restarting your device**: Restarting your device is one option when an Alexa error occurs. From your iPhone, long press the sleep/wake button until the option appears on your screen to restart. From an Android device, hold down your power button until the restart option appears on the screen.

2. **Force close the application**: From your iPhone, in order to force close an application, double press your Home button. A slider of open applications should appear on your screen. Swipe the Alexa app upward in order to close it.

    From your Android device, navigate to the *Settings* on your device and select *Apps* or *Applications*. Find Alexa in the list of installed applications. You have the option to clear data for your application if desired. Amazon recommends clearing the data and selecting *Force Stop*.

3. **Uninstall the Application**: From the Android device settings, select *Manage applications* and find Alexa in the listing of apps on your device. Select *Uninstall* in order to remove the application from your phone. Another way to uninstall the application from your Android device is to long press on the Alexa app from

your general applications section. Once the app is selected drag it to the top of the screen which should read *Uninstall* on the top left. From your iOS device, long press the Alexa application until it begins to shake on your screen. Once this happens tap the 'X' on the app.

After you have uninstalled the application navigate to your respective app store and re-download the application.

- Dot is not responding to the wake word "Alexa."

If you find that your Dot is not responding when you say "Alexa" and you have already completed the voice training, go into the Alexa app and ensure that your wake word is actually Alexa.

This can be done by simply opening the app, navigating to *Settings* and selecting *Wake Word*. Here, you can change the wake word to or from "Alexa."

- Dot is not finding my music or opening the correct application.

As an Alexa user you must always be specific in how you interact with her. There are a variety of commands that can be used to open, play, and change your music selections within the moment; however, if it is not spoken properly the Echo Dot will not know how to comply with your request.

Going through the Voice Training section of the application may also aid you in finding commands that you did not know how to use. Alexa requires specific instructions when playing music. Some examples may include the following:

- *"Play Chris Brown on Spotify."* This command shuffles music by this artist from Spotify. Omitting the application name will cause the command to fail and Alexa to become confused.

- *"Play Spotify."* This command simply plays music where you last left off.

If you have connected your personal music library or purchased music from the Digital Music Store you do not have to be as specific in your commands to Alexa. Simple commands may include:

- *"Alexa, play Chris Brown."*

- *"Alexa, shuffle Beyoncé."*

- *"Alexa, play the new Lady Gaga song."*

There are also a variety of commands that allow you to control your music. These include basic commands like *"Repeat this song," "Next song,"* or even *"Buy this song."*

Chapter 8: Troubleshooting Issues with Your Amazon Dot

Before you give up on your Amazon Echo Dot, make sure that you follow the needed steps to fix any issues you are having. The Dot is an innovative solution for the automation of not just your home but various aspects of your life. If you're having trouble, be sure to refer to this section to find some quick fixes to common issues you may be experiencing.

Your Amazon Echo Dot Ring

The ring around your Amazon Echo Dot will generally be your indicator that something is wrong. There are six different colors which may illuminate on the Dot's ring depending on the action.

Solid Blue and Cyan: These colors are used together in a variety of different scenarios. These scenarios happen after the wake word is spoken, during dispersing of the user's command, and throughout Alexa's response to your command. They also appear during the initial boot process of your Echo Dot.

Solid Red: A red indicator light means that you have placed your dot on Mute. This is done by selecting the mute button on the top of your device.

Orange Spinning Clockwise: The orange indicator light means that your device is attempting to connect to the wireless network.

White: A white light generally means you are adjusting the volume on your device.

Wavering Violet: Wavering violet lights generally indicate that an error has occurred during the setup of your wireless network.

If you are not able to successfully connect to your Wi-Fi, try the following steps:

- Attempt to connect to the network again.

- Ensure you are entering the correct password for your network.

- Use your other devices as testers. If they cannot connect to the Wi-Fi, there may be an actual problem with your connection.

- Attempt to update the firmware for your network device/router.

- Attempt to connect again away from any devices that may interfere with the connection like a microwave.

- Reset your router using the pinhole on its back. Wait for the device to completely power up. While waiting for the device to power up, reset your Echo Dot by unplugging the power adapter for three seconds.

Issues with Sound

If you are having issues with your Echo Dot's sound quality, don't give up on your Dot yet. There are some things that you can try to get the Echo Dot back on your side. One common issue is using your Echo Dot with an accent. Although this has been an issue, there is a way to get Alexa to understand and get acclimated to your voice. The second generation Echo Dot also features an updated language processer and is better at identifying user commands.

If you feel like Alexa is misconstruing your words, attempt to run the voice training program again. Be sure that when you re-run the training you are in the normal conditions in which you would be using the device. Never place your voice right next to the microphone when performing the training. If you generally speak to Alexa from a considerable distance away, perform your training at the same distance.

Turning off any background noise will also ensure that the Dot is picking up your voice specifically. It is good to remember that if voice training is done correctly on one Alexa device, it will work better on your other devices as well.

When the voice training starts, the ring around your Amazon Echo will illuminate and you will be prompted on your smart device to read through 25 sentences. If you feel as if you have said something wrong or that it wasn't clear, you can simply repeat your sentence before clicking *Next*.

After you complete the voice training process you have the option to complete the training again in order to further tune your results.

Issues with Alexa Discovering Your Smart Home Device

If you are having issues with your Echo Dot discovering your Smart Home device there are a number of things you can do in order to troubleshoot the connection.

First, ensure that your new home device is compatible with your Echo Dot. A supported list of devices can be found at https://www.amazon.com/alexasmarthome. If your home device is indeed on the list of supported items, the next step is double checking to determine if a "skill" is needed in order for it to work with Alexa. WeMo and Phillips are two brands who do not need "skills" in order for them to work with the Echo Dot.

Follow the steps below in order to properly troubleshoot your device.

- Download the companion application for your smart home device and proceed with the standalone setup.

- Ensure that your device is currently connected to the same Wi-Fi network as your Amazon Echo Dot.

- If an issue persists with your connection, try restarting both devices.

- Confirm that any software updates needed for the home device have been performed.

- Disable the skill associated with your home device and re-enable.

- Try discovering your devices again. Simply tell Alexa to *"Discover my devices"* in order to place the Amazon Echo Dot in discoverable mode.

Echo Dot is Not Responding or Does Not Turn On

If you are having issues with your Echo Dot responding or not turning on there are a variety of steps you can try in order to aid your device in becoming responsive again.

- The easiest way to troubleshoot this issue is to ensure that you are using the power adapter that comes with your devices. Cellular device chargers or other low level power adapters do not provide the needed power for the Echo Dot to operate accordingly.

- Use the Action button to determine if Alexa will respond. Once the button is pushed, attempt to speak your command to Alexa again.

- Ensure that when you are speaking to Alexa it is clear and natural. Also confirm that there is no background noise when speaking to Alexa.

- If you are using an external speaker, make sure your speaker is at least 3 feet away from the Echo Dot so that it does not interfere with sound quality. Make sure that it is at least 8 inches from a wall or various other objects.

Streaming Issues with the Echo Dot

Streaming issues with your Echo Dot are usually determined by your Wi-Fi connections. Look below to find ways to troubleshoot and rectify this issue.

- **Reduce Wi-Fi Congestion**: Reduce your Wi-Fi congestion by turning off devices that are not in use in order to free bandwidth on your network. If your device is close to the ground or on the floor, attempt to raise the device higher and move it away from any walls that may be blocking the signal. If the issue persists it may also help to move your device closer to the router/modem.

- **Reset Your Device**: In order to attempt to get rid of streaming issues, restart your Echo Dot as well as the modem. This is done by simply pressing and holding down the Microphone and Volume Down buttons simultaneously. This is done until the light ring on your device turns orange. Once complete, the light ring should turn blue then turn on and off again. Once this is complete, navigate to your Alexa application and set up your Wi-Fi again.

- **Restart Your Device**: In order to restart your Amazon Echo, unplug the power adapter from the wall or from the back of the device. Wait a few seconds and plug your device back in.

- **Restart Your Network Device**: If issues persist with the network connectivity of your device, try resetting your router or modem. This can be done by unplugging the network device or pressing the pin hole on the back of the network device. Once it is fully rebooted, allow your Echo Dot time to connect and retry your original action.

- **Contact Your Internet Service Provider**: If your problem persists and it is not an issue with your Echo Dot device, contact your Internet Service Provider for more help troubleshooting your network connection.

Bluetooth Connectivity Issues with Your Echo Dot

If you are having issues with your Echo Dot connecting to Bluetooth there are a number of steps that you can try in order to overcome these issues. These fixes may include the following:

- **Interference**: If your Bluetooth connectivity is not functioning as intended try moving your device away from anything that could potentially interfere with the connection. These interferences may include baby monitors, microwaves, or other wireless devices.

- **Battery Life**: The battery life of your device may also hinder your ability to connect via Bluetooth. If your device has a battery that cannot be removed make sure that it has a full charge. If your device has a removable and/or rechargeable batteries, replace or recharge the batteries.

- **Clear All Bluetooth Devices:** Clearing and reconnecting the Bluetooth device may aid in rectifying connectivity issues. In order to clear your Bluetooth device, navigate to *Settings* from the left navigation panel. Once inside of Settings, select your Alexa Device, select *Bluetooth* > *Clear*.

- **Pair a New Bluetooth Device**: The easiest way to test a Bluetooth device is to clear all devices and reconnect a new one. This can be done by selecting your Alexa device, selecting *Bluetooth* > *Pair a New Device*. Once your device enters pairing mode select the device from your cellular device. Alexa will let you know if your device has connected successfully.

-

Bluetooth Connectivity Issues with Your Echo Dot and the Alexa Voice Remote

If you are having issues with your Echo Dot connecting with your Alexa Voice Remote, there are some simple solutions that can be attempted in order to rectify this issue.

- **New Batteries**: Over time batteries tend to lose charge or corrode if they have been sitting for too long. Insert new AAA batteries in the correct orientations into your Alexa Voice Remote.

- **Pair Remote Again**: If you find that your device is not working properly with your Echo Dot go into your Alexa Dot settings, select the device which your remote is paired and select *Forget Remote*.

  Once your remote has been forgotten you can run through the device setup again with your Echo Dot and the Alexa Voice Remote.

- **Restart Your Echo Dot:** If nothing from the above options works for connecting your device, attempt to restart your device. Restarting your Echo is done by simply unplugging the power adapter from your device and plugging it back in.

Chapter 9: Amazon Echo Dot Vs. Everybody

For almost two years, Amazon has monopolized the home-based hub industry with the Amazon Echo, Amazon Tap, and the Amazon Echo Dot. Now its competitors are stepping up. Two of the major competitors against Amazon include the Google Home and Apple's innovations with Siri.

There are a number of alternatives, which are not as popular as the options by Google or Apple; however, no one can come close to the Amazon Echo in terms of price point.

Echo Dot (Generation 1) vs. Echo Dot (Generation 2)

The Echo Dot Second Generation builds upon the success of the first generation with enhanced features. Physically the most noticeable change in the new Echo Dot is its seemingly smaller size, even if only by a hair, and its use of volume buttons rather than the volume ring. The first generation Dot also contained a LED power light that the current one does not have. The second generation Echo Dot also does not come with the 3.5mm cable that was part of the original packaging of the first generation Echo Dot. The second generation Dot is also available in a white pearl color, which the first Dot was not.

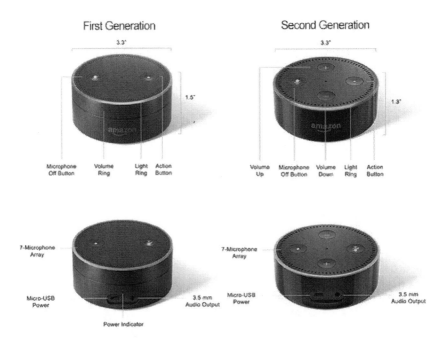

A lot of the specifications for the Echo Dot 1 and 2 remain similar; however, it is its internal workings which have changed. Although the Dot 2 does come with the same seven far-field microphones as the first design, a new speech processer was incorporated to enhance the speech accuracy on the new generation.

The second generation device also adds the Echo Spatial Perception or ESP. This add-on ensures that in a home with multiple Alexa devices, only a single one will respond. Even though this was not included with the first generation suite of Alexa devices, they will get the ESP soon through a software update.

The Echo Dot First Generation also received lots of criticism for only being available to a select audience with limited quantities. Originally it was only available to order via an Alexa device. Amazon has since made this device more available to its consumers via the Amazon website as well as Best Buy in select areas. Amazon has also dropped the price point for the Echo Dot Second Generation by nearly half the amount of the first which was available for $89.99. It is now available for $49.99. With the slashing of the price, they have also slashed the length of the warranty available to users dropping the original 1-year warranty to only 90 days.

Echo Dot vs. Google Home

The Google Home is Amazon's newest competitor against its suite of Alexa products. Compared to the Dot priced at $49, the Google Home comes in at a substantially higher price point of $130. Much like how Google interacts with a cellular device, the Home awakens using the keyword *"Okay Google."* Although Google attempts to win in the design battle with its customizable base, the Echo Dot is also available in two colors as well as having various fabric cases to change the Dot's style. Google has not mentioned much about the Home in terms of its integration with smart home products, which is an area that the Alexa products do very well.

Echo Dot vs. Apple

Apple, although not officially a competitor, is always looking for ways to strike in various technology-focused markets. Even though Apple has not officially announced the release of a home-based system, they are readily making Siri available to welcome the change.

Apple recently opened the SDK for Siri. This is significant because developers are now able to build Siri's voice command functionality to their applications. Uber is one company who has been gearing up for the change. Recently, they announced that users would shortly be able to use voice commands in order to book rides with Uber. A home application was also released by Apple, which is in conjunction with Apple's Homekit platform. This application is used to control various HomeKit smart home appliances.

Being that the Echo Dot is a standalone device that doesn't require direct interaction with a user's cellular device, it is still quite ahead of Apple in this area. Estimations of an Apple-like home product would be on the high end of the price point nearing $300.

Feedbacks of Real Users

Jessica: This device is getting smarter all the time. It's easy to add skills. It's very impressive.

David: It's an excellent product. Usually we use it to control our TP-Link smart home devices and it works perfect. We also ask Alexa to play music. I really recommend it to everybody who wants smart home functionality.

Christopher: I've got two original models of Echo Dot. And the new Echo Dot is almost the same like original except it cannot maintain an internet connection. I put the old and the new model in the same place and the news one drops the connection at least 2 times per day while the original never has such problems. I made an experiment with other two new models, using them side by side. And it was the same problem. I don't think these are defective units. Very disappointed.

The rest is just great. Echo Dot is a very functional and smart device.

Brandon: This small device is packed with wonderful Alexa apps. Alexa is a great assistant. It helps with shopping list, weather forecast, news and everyday items.

Emily: I was a little skeptical about purchasing the Echo Dot (2nd Generation) but now I am pleased with my purchase. I put it in my bedroom and I like when it plays music until I fall asleep. I also bought a second Dot for my basement as I spent my laundry day there. I can ask about anything my Dot if I get bored. I also have Amazon Echo which is in my living room. I am very happy I've got these devices. They have brought a lot of fun and they work perfect. I recommend both products to anyone.

Audrey: The Echo Dot is ok. But I don't like that Alexa has terrible search feature. When I ask such kind of questions like "what time does Saturday night live come on", she doesn't know the answer. She answers only 3 of 10 questions I ask while google or Siri have no this problem. I am a little upset.

Joseph: Honestly, I am very impressed with Echo Dot. I've got a big family. And now everybody in our family has his own Dot. My children like playing with them, asking questions. They also use it while doing their homework. My wife uses it for music, weather and listening to the latest new. And I use it for everything. I would write lots of review to support this product. It's just awesome.

Julia: I got Echo as a gift a few months ago and it's surprising for me how much I use it. It has become a part of my life. I was a little skeptical about buying Echo Dot and I took one to try out. Now I want to order a bunch more. This device works nicely and it sound pretty good for its size. I put my Dot in my bathroom and I plan to Bluetooth it to a set of speaker. The sound is great in the bathroom. I am going to make a full smart home system with tp-links and plugs and switches.

I suggest buying 3 or 6 Echo Dots just to save your money. Because when you try this you'll want more.

Conclusion

Size, versatility, and intelligence are three things you should look for when purchasing a device like the Amazon Echo Dot. With only a few other options in its class it's no wonder why people are falling in love with the Amazon Echo Dot (second generation).

As part of the Alexa family, the Echo Dot is only one in a line of many devices with the ability to speak to Alexa. Alexa provides the versatility needed to make the Amazon Echo Dot the perfect home control device. Not only do you have the ability to control home devices, Alexa keeps any needed information at your fingertips.

Are you running late and unsure of the weather? Ask Alexa.

Are you unsure of what traffic looks like on your commute to work? Ask Alexa.

Are you hungry and in need of your favorite Domino's pizza? Ask Alexa.

Alexa on your Echo Dot is more than a virtual assistant—she's a life manager. She keeps you organized, prepared, on time, and entertained. With the ability to learn, Alexa will only continue to get smarter. With each command and skill update you will continue to realize why the Amazon Alexa-enabled devices are dominating the home hub market. For these devices and the Echo Dot in particular, competitors are few and far between.

A sleek design, a small package, and a big brain all describe the Amazon Echo Dot Second Generation. Whether you have one, two or even six devices, the Echo Dot will definitely continue to serve its intended purpose and so much more.

Thank you for reading. I hope you enjoy it. I ask you to leave your honest feedback.

I think next books will also be interesting for you:

Amazon Tap

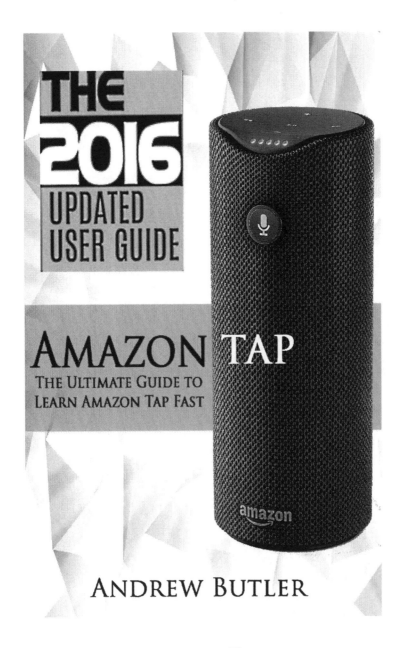

Amazon Dot

Amazon Fire TV

Amazon Fire TV

Amazon Echo

Windows 10

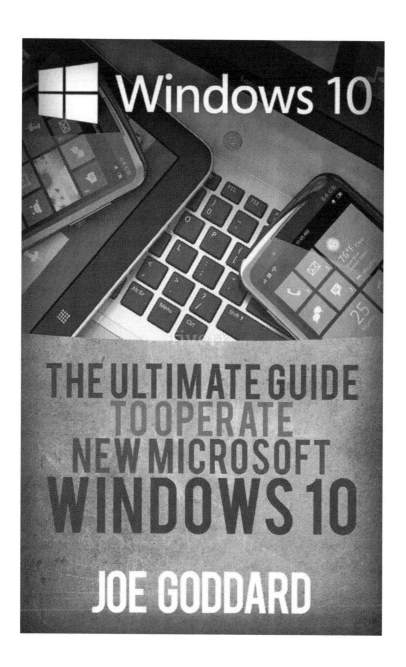